STUART LITTLE

by
E. B. White

Teacher Guide

Written by
Anne Troy

D1379156

Note

The Harper Trophy paperback edition of the book was used to prepare this guide. The page references may differ in the hardcover or other paperback editions.

Please note: Please assess the appropriateness of this book for the age level and maturity of your students prior to reading and discussing it with your class.

ISBN 1-56137-452-0

To order, contact your local school supply store, or—

Novel Units, Inc.
P.O. Box 433
Bulverde, TX 78163-0433

Web site: www.educyberstor.com

Table of Contents

Chapters contain: Vocabulary Words
and Activities, Discussion Questions and
Activities, Predictions, Supplementary Activities

Skills and Strategies

Thinking
Brainstorming, visualization,
classifying and categorizing,
synthesizing, analyzing

Comprehension
Predicting, sequencing,
cause/effect, drawing conclusions, decision making

Writing
Journal, narrative, letter,
descriptive, comparison/
contrast

Vocabulary
Context clues, antonyms/
synonyms

Listening/Speaking
Participation in discussion,
drama, cooperative groups

Literary Elements
Characterization, setting,
plot development, conflict,
theme, mood/tone, point of
view, imagery

Summary

Stuart Little is a pleasant, personable mouse who is born into a human family. His size—just over two inches tall—presents challenges and adventures for the young Little. E. B. White provides us with the delightful story.

About the Author

E. B. White was born in Mt. Vernon, New York, and was graduated from Cornell University. He wrote many books for children and adults including *Charlotte's Web* and *The Trumpet of the Swan*.

Introductory Information and Activities

Instructions Prior to Reading

You may wish to choose one or more of the following Prereading Activities. Each is designed to help students draw from their store of background knowledge about the events and themes they will meet in the story they are about to read.

Prereading Activities

1. Previewing: Have students examine the title and cover illustration. Also suggest that they flip through the book. Note that the illustrator is Garth Williams. He is the illustrator of *Charlotte's Web*.

2. What is unusual about the illustration? Can you find any clues about the story? the characters? the type of story?

3. Read the first four paragraphs of the book aloud to the class. Measure two inches with a ruler. Give each student a two inch long piece of colored paper. Brainstorm challenges Stuart might encounter. Keep the list posted while you are working on the novel.

4. List what students already know about mice. Use the K-W-L visual to help students' comprehension (see below). (Carr, Eileen and Ogle, Donna, 1987, "K-W-L Plus: A Strategy for Comprehension and Summarization." *Journal of Reading*, 30 (7) 626-631.)

What I Know	What I Want to Find Out	What I Learned

5. Introduce the "Mouse Center Activities" found at the end of the unit on page 24.

6. Real Versus Make-Believe: Read the back cover of the book to the class. Is this going to be a make-believe story or a realistic story? How do you know? Use the T-chart to discuss.

	Realistic Story	**Make-Believe Story**
Setting:	Our world	Not quite our world
Characters:	Like us	Unusual
Action:	Could happen	Could never happen
Problem:	Could be ours	Couldn't be ours

Bulletin Board Activities
1. Have students create a bulletin board display depicting the characters they meet in the book, complete with the clothing or props which identify each.

2. Display other book jackets by E. B. White, such as *Charlotte's Web* and *The Trumpet of the Swan*. "*Stuart Little* is like_____." As the book is read, add class responses.

Recommended Procedure
Teachers are encouraged to adapt the guide to meet the needs of individual classes and students. You know your students best. Do not feel that you have to use everything in the guide —pick and choose. We are offering you some tools for working. Here are some of the "nuts and bolts" for using these "tools"—a glossary of some of the terms used that will facilitate your use and understanding of the guide.

Blooms' Taxonomy: a classification system for various levels of thinking. Questions keyed to these levels may be

• Comprehension questions, which ask one to state the meaning of what is written;

• Application questions, which ask one to think about relationships between ideas such as cause/effect;

• Evaluation questions, which ask one to judge the accuracy of ideas; and

• Synthesis questions, which ask one to develop a product by integrating the ideas in the text with ideas of one's own.

Graphic Organizers
Visual representation of how ideas are related to each other. These "pictures"—including Venn diagrams, flow charts, attribute webs, etc.—help students collect information, make interpretations, solve problems, devise plans, and become aware of how they think.

Cooperative Learning

Learning activities in which groups of two or more students collaborate. There is compelling research evidence that integration of social activities into the learning process—such as small group discussion, group editing, group art projects—often leads to richer, more long-lasting learning.

This book will be read one chapter at a time, using DRTA (Directed Reading Thinking Activity) method. This technique involves reading a section, predicting what will happen next, making good guesses based on what has already occurred in the story. The students continue to read and everyone verifies the prediction.

Before reading a chapter, specific vocabulary words will be pointed out to the students. A variety of vocabulary activities will be suggested.

After reading a chapter, the class will brainstorm "what ifs." What if one or another character wasn't in the story, a character did something different, events followed a different sequence or didn't happen at all, etc. The teacher writes all these "what if" class responses on the board or a large sheet of paper. At the conclusion of the novel, the review of these "what ifs" may be used in writing a different development and/or an ending for the novel.

Prereading Discussion Questions

Mice and cats: Why do mice infest some houses and not others? What would be an "ideal home" for mice? What are some ways to get rid of mice? Which would you use if you had a problem with mice? Can you think of some unusual new ways?

Facing danger: What are some of the dangers we have to face today? Have you ever had to face personal danger? How do people react to danger? Can you think of examples of people who have found extra courage when they needed it? What do these examples have in common?

Being small: What are some special problems that short people face? What are some ways of coping with these problems? Are there any advantages?

Using Predictions

We all make predictions as we read—little guesses about what will happen next, how the conflict will be resolved, which details given by the author will be important to the plot, which details will help to fill in our sense of a character. Students should be encouraged to predict, to make sensible guesses. As students work on predictions, these discussion questions can be used to guide them: What are some of the ways to predict? What is the process of a sophisticated reader's thinking and predicting? What clues does an author give us to help us in making our predictions? Why are some predictions more likely than others?

A predicting chart is for students to record their predictions. As each subsequent chapter is discussed, you can review and correct previous predictions. This procedure serves to focus on predictions and to review the stories.

Use the facts and ideas the author gives.

Use your own knowledge.

Use new information that may cause you to change your mind.

Predictions:

_____

_____

_____

_____

Prediction Chart

What characters have we met so far?	What is the conflict in the story?	What are your predictions?	Why did you make those predictions?

Vocabulary
shinnying 2   solemnly 3   horrified 4
trifle 5

Vocabulary Activity
The students will develop word maps. They will use color to distinguish antonyms and synonyms. For words that have clear antonyms, the following framework is suitable:

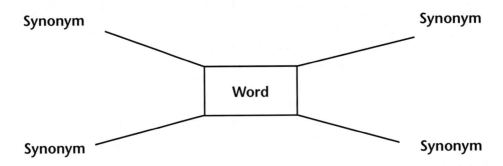

This may be an individual or cooperative group activity. Students might enjoy coming up with variations on this framework. For example, instead of listing antonyms, students could provide line drawings to illustrate the target word. The word maps should be displayed.
Cooperative Learning Activity: You may want to have all students examine examples of word maps for all vocabulary words, even when the list is too lengthy to expect one student to map all the words. One way to circumvent the problem is to assign small groups responsibility for several words; each group selects a reporter who explains the group's word maps to the large group, using an overhead projector.

Discussion Questions and Activities
1. Who is the main character? Begin an attribute web for Stuart. (See page 9 of this guide.)

2. Where do the Littles live? *(Page 3, New York City)*

3. What special arrangement did the Littles make for Stuart because of his size? *(Page 2, They made him a tiny bed out of clothes pins and a cigarette box. Mrs. Little made him a special little suit.)*

4. How did Stuart help with the lost ring? *(Page 5, Stuart went down the drain after the ring.)*

5. What was funny in this chapter?

Prediction
What adventures will Stuart have? Is he really a member of the Little family?

Using Character Webs

Attribute Webs are simply a visual representation of a character from the novel. They provide a systematic way for the students to organize and recap the information they have about a particular character. Attribute webs may be used after reading the novel to recapitulate information about a particular character or completed gradually as information unfolds, done individually, or finished as a group project.

One type of character attribute web uses these divisions:
• How a character acts and feels. (How does the character feel in this picture? How would you feel if this happened to you? How do you think the character feels?)

• How a character looks. (Close your eyes and picture the character. Describe him to me.)

• Where a character lives. (Where and when does the character live?)

• How others feel about the character. (How does another specific character feel about our character?)

In group discussion about the student attribute webs and specific characters, the teacher can ask for backup proof from the novel. You can also include inferential thinking.
Attribute webs need not be confined to characters. They may also be used to organize information about a concept, object, or place.

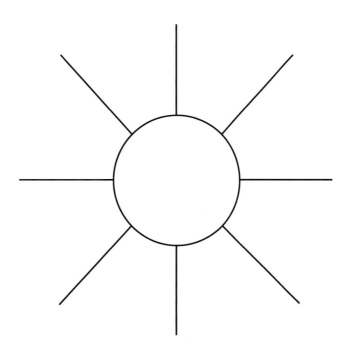

Supplementary Activities

1. Writing: Begin a journal in which you react to each section of the story you read. Reactions might include: Questions you have about the story; memories the story evokes; people or other stories of whom characters remind you; judgments about whether you agree or disagree with what characters have done; your thoughts about topics which come up, such as fear, courage, heroism, etc. Try sometimes including vocabulary words from the story in your journal.

2. Writing: Imagine that you wake up one morning to find that you are only two inches tall! Write a composition about some of the problems you would have, and how you might solve them. (What would you do about clothing, food, shelter, entertainment, or threats to your safety?)

3. Math: How tall is the average third grader? How much taller is a third grader in comparison to Stuart? Convert the height of the average third grader to inches. How many "two inches" will it take to equal the height of a third grader? How tall is the average father? Take the heights given by the class. Find the average. Convert the average father's height to inches and again how many "two inches" it will take to equal the height of a father. Make a large chart to display the results.

4. Story Map: A story map is an outline that helps you to understand and remember the story better. Many stories have the same parts—a setting, a problem, a goal, and a series of events that lead up to an ending or conclusion. These story elements can be placed on a story map. Just as a road map leads a driver from one place to another, so too, a story map leads a reader from one point to another. What do you know about the story after reading only the first chapter?

   • What is the setting?

   • Who is the main character?

   • What is the problem?

   As the story is read, more characters may be added and the setting and the problem may change, so additions may be made. (See page 11 of this guide.)

5. Art: Make a family portrait of the Little family.

Story Map

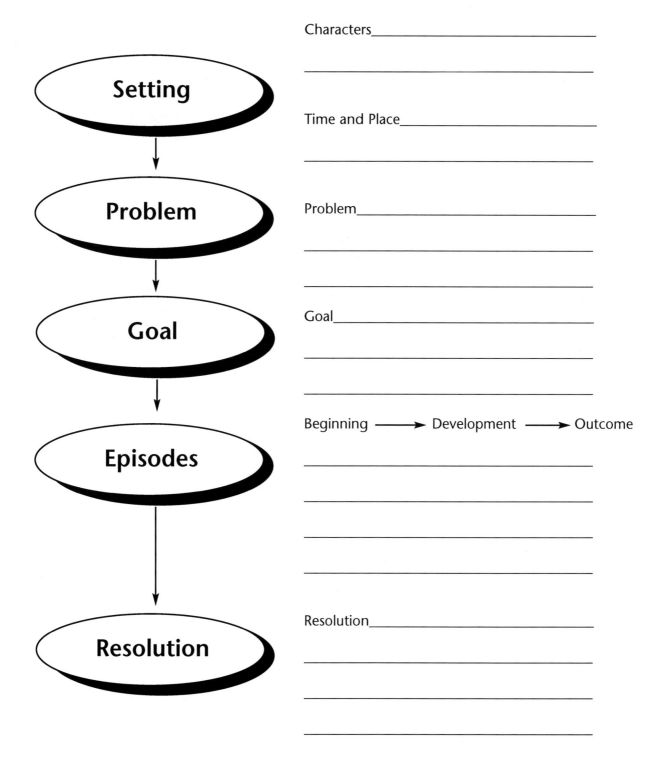

Setting

Characters_____

_____

Time and Place_____

_____

Problem

Problem_____

_____

_____

Goal

Goal_____

_____

_____

Episodes

Beginning ———▶ Development ———▶ Outcome

_____

_____

_____

Resolution

Resolution_____

_____

_____

_____

Chapter II   "Home Problems"—Pages 7-11

Vocabulary

inconvenience 8   emerge 9   belittling 10
venture 11

Vocabulary Activity

Before Reading: List the vocabulary words on the board or on a sheet of paper in the form of a table. Pronounce the words. Ask the students to rate their knowledge of each of the words as a group or individually.

	I Can Define	I Have Heard	I Don't Know
Words:			

After Reading: How many words are in the "I Don't Know" column? What are different ways to learn and remember these words? Brainstorm.

Discussion Questions and Activities

1. What did you learn about Stuart in this chapter? What characteristics can you add to his attribute web?

2. Why were the parents protective of Stuart? *(Pages 9-11)*

3. The Littles were concerned about the word "mice" in songs and sayings. Why? What word would you use instead?

4. Why was the father worried about the mousehole? *(Page 11, He feared that Stuart would venture into it.)*

5. If Stuart were your brother, how could he help you?

Prediction

Do you think Stuart will ever go into the mousehole?

Supplementary Activities

1. Start two lists—first, the ways Stuart acts like a human, and secondly, the ways Stuart acts like a mouse.

2. Comparisons: What other books have you read about mice? How is this book alike or different from the others? Discuss with your classmates.

Chapter III   "Washing Up"—Pages 12-16

Vocabulary

abdominal 13	wool wrapper 13	friar 14
bellrope 14	abbey 14	washbasin 14
brace 15	brad-awl 15	blacksmith 16

Vocabulary Activity
Ask students to "guess" at the meaning of the day's words from context, telling why for each guess. Make a list of the "why answers" to teach context clues.

Discussion Questions and Activities
1. Setting: What was the time of day/year in Chapter III? *(Not specified, but students may refer to page 13, "In wintertime it would be quite dark...")*

2. How did Stuart manage to care for himself? *(Pages 14-16, Stuart could wash himself with doll-size soap, and the toothbrush and toothpaste provided by Mrs. Little. George rigged up a brace so Stuart could use the washbasin.)*

3. Identify Stuart's problem in Chapter III. How is his problem solved? *(Page 16, He could not turn on the faucet to wash his face or brush his teeth. He used a light hammer made of wood and swung it three times around his head and let it come down with a crash against the handle of the faucet, and started a thin stream of water flowing.)*

4. What do you think George thought of Stuart? *(pages 4-5, 8, 15)*

5. Were there any incidents that were funny? Why?

Supplementary Activities
1. At the end of each chapter list the major event in the chapter on the story map.

2. Stuart had problems because he was so little. Suppose Stuart found a magic ring and he rubbed it twice and became 10 feet tall. Write a story telling what happened to Stuart when he was 10 feet tall. What were some of the advantages? What would be dangerous for him? What wouldn't he be able to do? Do you think Stuart would rather be two inches tall or 10 feet tall?

3. How tall do you think Stuart is in metric measurements? *(two inches = 5.08 centimeters)*

4. Make a cartoon showing the major events of Chapter III.

Vocabulary

       acrobats 19   mackerel 19

Discussion Questions and Activities

1. Why was Snowbell irritated with Stuart? *(Page 17, Stuart made so much noise trying to get the water started that he awakened everyone.)*

2. Why do you think Snowbell showed his two rows of gleaming white teeth to Stuart? *(Page 18, to frighten him)*

3. Compare Stuart's size of two inches to the average length of a grown cat. How many inches longer is the cat?

4. Why did Stuart grab the shade ring? *(Pages 18-19, Stuart tried to show off, as an acrobat might do, with the window shade.)*

5. How did Snowbell and Stuart react to each other? Research: Do all cats try to catch and eat mice?

6. Why did Snowbell put Stuart's hat and cane in front of the mousehole? *(Page 20, to hint that Stuart had gone down the mousehole like the Littles had worried)*

Prediction

Will Stuart be rescued and how?

Supplementary Activity

Investigate how a window shade works. Could a two-inch mouse really be rolled up in a window shade?

Vocabulary

vigorous 21   pry 21   disgust 23
discarded 24   exasperated 25   idiotic 25

Vocabulary Activity

Make a synonym chain for each of the vocabulary words. The first one is an example.

Vigorous—strong—active—robust—sturdy—healthy—hale—energetic—forceful

Discussion Questions and Activities:

1. George's suggestions for rescuing Stuart were not kindly received by his parents. *(page 21)* What do you think George really thought of Stuart? How would you like a brother two inches tall? Tell why.

2. George tried to put applesauce down the mousehole. What kind of food do you think might have been a better rescue food?

3. Why did the man at the Bureau of Missing Persons hang up in disgust? *(Page 23, He probably thought that Mr. Little was a bit crazy.)*

4. How was Stuart found? *(Page 25, George started to pull down all the shades because that is one custom of showing respect for the dead. George pulled a cord of a shade and out popped Stuart.)*

5. Why were Stuart's hat and cane found at the entrance to the mousehole? *(Page 25, Snowbell had put them there.)* What does Stuart mean when he says, "...you can draw your own conclusions"?

Prediction

What kinds of adventures do you think Stuart will have?

Vocabulary

inconvenience 28	fare 29	spectacles 29
sloops 30	schooners 30	mainmast 31
bow 32	foredeck 32	berth 32
diminutive 32	prow 33	squall 33
squid 33	jib 33	jibe 33
luff 33	leech 33	blunder 33
detestable 33	capsizing 34	yawing 34
deck cleat 34		

Vocabulary Activity
Match the following definitions and the vocabulary list.

1. _____ Erratically go from side to side of a course *(yawing)*

2. _____ A sea mollusk with no shell *(squid)*

3. _____ A sailing boat with one mast, a fore-and-aft rig, and a single jib *(sloop)*

4. _____ The bow of a ship *(prow)*

5. _____ To sail a ship closer to the wind *(luff)*

6. _____ An avoidable and usually serious mistake *(blunder)*

7. _____ Indicating small size *(diminutive)*

Discussion Questions and Activities:
1. Were there any unrealistic things in this chapter?

2. What kind of boats were in the story? *(toy boats)* How can you prove this? *(Page 30, They were sailing in Central Park in New York.)*

3. Do you think Stuart was an experienced sailor? Why or why not?

Prediction
Will Stuart be able to beat the sloop in a race?

Supplementary Activity
Locate Central Park on a map of New York City.

Chapter VII   "The Sailboat Race"—Pages 36-46

Vocabulary

referee 38	cresting 39	consternation 39	barometer 41
flotsam 41	ominous 41	rigging 43	staysail 44
halyards 44	southard 45	helm 45	

Vocabulary Activity

Place the words for the day in categories, e.g.,

Descriptive Sailing Words	Feelings	Actions	Things	People
cresting rigging staysail halyards helm	consternation ominous		flotsam barometer	referee

Discussion Questions and Activities

1. How did the policeman affect the sailboat race? *(Page 39, The policeman fell into the pond and caused a great wave which overwhelmed the boats.)*

2. What was "dirty weather"? How did it affect Stuart and the Wasp? *(Page 41, Stormy weather; it made sailing more dangerous.)*

3. Why did the owner roar, "Cut away all paper bags"? *(Page 44, The Wasp had sailed into a floating empty sack which kept the boat from sailing on.)*

4. What is an understatement? *(An understatement is a statement with restraint, especially for great effect.)* Find an example of understatement in this chapter. *(Page 46, "When Stuart got home that night, his brother George asked him where he had been all day. 'Oh, knocking around town,' replied Stuart.")*

Vocabulary

tapioca 47	penetrate 48	bronchitis 49	vireo 50
scientifically 50	vales 51	shinnied 54	

Vocabulary Activity

In cooperative groups make bingo cards using the vocabulary words from all the chapters read. The cards may be added to as the book is read. The caller of the game may use the vocabulary words or the word definitions.

Discussion Questions and Activities

1. How did Stuart get bronchitis? *(Page 48, He was trapped in the cold refrigerator.)*

2. Who was Margalo? How did she happen to be in the Little household? *(Page 50, Mrs. Little noticed a small bird lying on the windowsill, apparently dead. She brought it in and revived it.)*

3. Why and who did Stuart fear would hurt or kill the bird? *(page 53, Snowbell)* If Snowbell did not harm Stuart, why should Snowbell be tempted to harm Margalo?

4. Why was it lucky that George gave Stuart a bow and arrow during his illness? *(Page 55, He was able to protect Margalo from the wicked Snowbell.)*

Prediction

Do you think Snowbell will get even with Stuart?

Supplementary Activity

Make up a tick-tack-toe board that would be appropriate for Stuart and Mrs. Little.

Vocabulary

scow 60   slithering 60   tuft 63   perish 64
buoys 66

Vocabulary Activity

For each of the vocabulary words write a sentence that makes sense. Omit the vocabulary word. Make an answer key on the back of the paper. Share your sentences with a classmate.

Discussion Questions and Activities

1. How did Stuart get involved with garbage? *(Pages 57-58, He jumped into a garbage can to avoid the Irish terrier, and the garbage can was dumped into a truck.)*

2. Why did Stuart cry? *(Page 61, "The thought of death made Stuart sad...")*

3. Who saved Stuart? How? *(Pages 61-63, Margalo helped by letting Stuart grab her feet and flew him out of the garbage and back to the city.)*

4. What parallels do you see between Chapters VIII and IX? *(In Chapter VIII, Stuart saved Margalo from Snowbell. In Chapter IX, Margalo saved Stuart from sure death in the dumping of garbage in the ocean.)*

Supplementary Activity

Writing: How does E. B. White describe garbage? Write two sentences of your own describing garbage.

Chapter X   "Springtime"—Pages 67-71

Vocabulary
delicatessen 67   offhand 69

Discussion Questions and Activities
1. Who were Snowbell's friends? *(page 67, other cats)*

2. What was their plot? *(Page 69, Although Snowbell really couldn't kill the bird or mouse who shared a home with him at the Littles, there was no reason that another cat couldn't and so the Angora made plans to do just that.)*

3. How was the plot foiled? *(Page 71, The pigeon overheard the plan and left a note warning Margalo.)*

Supplementary Activities
1. Diagraming/Thinking: How were the animals in this story unique? Prepare an attribute web.

2. Writing: The pigeon sent a note to Margalo. What kind of a note might you send to a pet? Write the warning the pigeon might have sent.

Chapter XI   "The Automobile"—Pages 72-82

Vocabulary

pariah 72	jauntily 75	pincers 78	miniature 78
extracting 78	crumpled 82	punctured 82	

Vocabulary Activity
Make a vocabulary activity for a classmate. Use more than the vocabulary from just one chapter. Pick five words and write synonyms. Arrange the words and synonyms so they may be matched. Write an answer key.

Discussion Questions and Activities
1. How did Stuart react to Margalo flying away? *(Page 72, Stuart was heartbroken and decided to run away and look for Margalo.)*

2. To whom did Stuart go for advice? *(Page 75, Dr. Carey, owner of the schooner Wasp)*

3. Why did Mr. Clydesdale talk so funny? *(Page 76, because his mouth was filled with gauze)*

4. What was special about Dr. Carey's miniature car? *(Page 79, It could become invisible.)*

5. How did Stuart and Dr. Carey find the miniature car? *(Page 82, by crawling around on their hands and knees)*

Chapter XII

Vocabulary

accessories 83	rhinestones 85	togs 86	stalked 87
nimbly 87	abomination 90	expectancy 91	objectionable 94
underprivileged 94	exertion 97		

Vocabulary Activity

Ask students to "guess" at the meaning of the day's words from context, telling why for each guess. Make a list of the "why" answers to teach context clues. Verify the "why" answers by using the dictionary.

Discussion Questions and Activities

1. Where did Stuart buy new clothes? *(Page 83, a doll shop)* How would you feel about being forced to buy clothes at a special store because of your size? Did Stuart seem to have problems accepting his limitations?

2. Who was "seated in thought by the side of the road"? *(Page 84, the Superintendent of Schools)* What does a superintendent of schools do? Can you name the superintendent of your school? Have you ever seen him/her? Where is the superintendent's office?

3. How was Stuart different from most substitutes? *(Pages 88-96, Answers will vary: Stuart was smaller; he did not follow the school routine; he kept order; the children obeyed him; Stuart led a discussion that most teachers would not approve of; Stuart dismissed class early.)*

4. What did the students learn from the Chairman of the World discussion? *(Answers will vary. What is important; good laws for the world.)*

Supplementary Activities

1. Dramatize the schoolroom scene.

2. Comparison: How does Stuart explain the difference between advice and law? Make a list of each using a T-chart.

ADVICE	LAW

3. Writing: Stuart says, "Summertime is important. It's like a shaft of sunlight" (page 98). Think of other ways to finish the quote. Write down two ways to finish, "Summertime is important. It's like_____."

Vocabulary

sarsaparilla 100	ruinous 102	prominent 104	ancestors 104
stamen 106	slunk 108	proportions 108	annoyances 110
tranquil 110	architects 110	muster 110	thwarts 112

Vocabulary Activity

Each student or cooperative group will make a poster, banner, or sign to advertise their word or words. The ad must show what the word means and how to pronounce it. The words will be displayed and should be signed by the artist(s).

Discussion Questions and Activities

1. How did the storekeeper describe Harriet Ames? *(pages 103-104, young, pretty, about Stuart's size, beautifully dressed, from a prominent family)*

2. When Stuart saw Harriet, what did he do? *(Pages 106-107, He began to tremble from excitement. He hid behind an inkwell.)*

3. How was Stuart's letter to Harriet funny? *(Page 109, Answers will vary. "My only drawback is that I look something like a mouse.")*

4. Describe Stuart's canoe and paddles. *(Page 111)*

Prediction

Do you think the boat will be waterproof? Will it leak? Will Stuart treat the canoe before he takes Harriet for a ride?

Chapter XIV   "An Evening on the River"—Pages 113-124

Vocabulary
ballasted 114   courteous 119   astern 122

Discussion Questions and Activities
1. What problems did Stuart find with the canoe? What repairs did he make? *(Pages 113-114, The boat leaked and it was a tippy boat. Stuart plugged the seams with spruce gum and "ballasted the canoe with stones until it floated evenly and steadily.")*

2. E. B. White said that the day of Stuart's date "dawned cloudy." *(page 117)* What did that phrase suggest about what will happen? What really did happen?

Supplementary Activities
1. Comparison Writing: Stuart had an idea of his evening with Harriet in his imagination. How was the real event different?

Imagined Evening	Real Event

2. Writing: Describe in a short paragraph a time when your expectations and reality differed.

Chapter XV   "Heading North"—Pages 125-131

Vocabulary
spurs 127   salute 127   rank 129   junipers 129

Vocabulary Activity
The teacher (or student) gives a definition and a student supplies the word. The game is played like a spelling bee. Use the words from the entire book or the last five chapters. This may be played in cooperative groups with the student teacher(s) using an answer key.

Discussion Questions and Activities
1. What adventure did Stuart have with the filling station man? *(pages 125-126, convincing the man to sell him 5 drops of gas)* What do you think he paid for this amount of gas?

2. What did Stuart and the telephone repairman talk about? *(pages 127-131, what one could see on travels to the north, southwest, or to the east)*

Post-reading Questions and Activities

1. Theme: What was the author's message? Why do you think the author wrote this story? What do you think is the most important thing to remember about this story?

2. Story Ending: Were you satisfied with the last chapter of the novel? Why or why not?

3. Complete the story map. How many episodes were there? What was the problem of the story and was it resolved?

4. Plot: Choose three events in the story, and write two or three paragraphs about how changing these events would have changed what happened in the story.

5. Character: Make a list of six adjectives that describe Stuart and include something from the story to show why you chose each adjective.

6. Make a collage about Stuart. You may use magazine cutouts and drawings of your own.

Mouse Center Activities

1. Famous Mice: How many mice can you list that have been made famous in cartoons, TV, movies, songs, or books?

2. How do mice communicate? Write an imaginary mouse conversation. Try to use quotation marks and correct punctuation.

3. Fables are fictitious stories that teach a lesson. The characters are often animals. Try writing a fable with a mouse as the main character.

4. Design a mouse game for mice to play. Describe your game, the rules, and any materials necessary so the game can be played.

5. Design an imaginary "mouse house." Make a mouse puppet and then write a short play with a mouse star.

6. Be a mouse for a day. What would you do? How would you feel? What would you eat? Decide on your size, color, etc. Where would you live? What will be on your mind? What will you fear? After you have thought about being a mouse, write a story to share with the class.

7. Make up mouse jokes and riddles. Read them to your friends.

8. What kind of people do mice like? Are there any animals that are friendly to mice? Pretend you are a mouse. What people or animals do you associate with? Share your tale with friends and discuss their reactions to your story.

9. Do all mice, large and small, have certain characteristics in common? Think about the characteristics of mice and what you know or feel about mice from your experiences with them. What are some characteristics or general traits that people associate with mice? *(whiskers, tails, hair, claws, tongues, teeth, eyes, etc.)*